A Tree Called Oscar

G.K. JONES

LifeRich Publishing is a registered trademark of The Reader's Digest Association, Inc.

LifeRich Publishing books may be ordered through booksellers or by contacting:

LifeRich Publishing
1663 Liberty Drive
Bloomington, IN 47403
www.liferichpublishing.com
1 (888) 238-8637

ISBN: 978-1-4897-0656-0 (sc)
ISBN: 978-1-4897-0657-7 (hc)
ISBN: 978-1-4897-0655-3 (e)

Print information available on the last page.

LifeRich Publishing rev. date: 03/04/2016

LifeRich
PUBLISHING®

Dedicated to

Lily, Jacob, and Hannah Rose

A Tree Called Oscar shows the importance of involved parents, friends, and compromise in life. It has wonderful illustrations, and shows a lot of love.

James Adelstein

Author of Two Brothers

What a blessing for any child who reads A Tree Called Oscar. It's full of love, happiness and joy, and is beautifully illustrated.

Dr. Beverly J Gaard Ph.d

Author of I Was There

This is a story about a tree called Oscar. It traces his progression from infancy to maturity. It shows the importance of nurturing parents and friends and of learning to adapt to lifes' difficulties. Everyone learns to compromise for the sake of each others' happiness.

One day at the edge of a woodland, two trees looked up and saw each other.

"Hello", said the larger tree.

"My name is Otis Walnut".

Blushing, the other tree said, "My name is Jenny Walnut".

"Oh, you're a walnut too! How wonderful!," said Otis.

As they grew, they fell in love and got married.

After a year, they decided to have a baby. "Where shall we plant the seed?" asked Mrs. Walnut. I think it should be close so we can look after it".

"But not so close that it won't have room to grow", said Mr. Walnut. "It shall be the grandest walnut in the countryside!"

They chose to plant their largest seed which grew inside their heart.

They asked Willie, the squirrel, if he would plant their special seed on the mound that rose from the meadow so that all the forest could watch it grow.

Willie planted the seed as his friends watched.

The following spring, Baby Walnut was born! All the little creatures of the forest gave him a birth party: his name was Oscar.

When he was about 4 inches tall, Oscar suddenly felt cold. He was shivering, when he heard his mother say "It's snowing! Oh dear, he was born too soon! He's going to die!". Her words were heard by Willie and his friend, Sam. "We must cover him!", said Willie.

They scurried to find something to cover little Oscar.

Finally, Oscar was safe.

Exhausted, Willie and Sam ran to Sams' house to get out of the cold, and fell fast asleep.

Little Oscar began to grow and soon stood 14 inches tall! He was very happy on the mound with all his little friends.

One day a young fawn walked up and began to nibble on Oscars' tender leaves.

Mrs. Walnut cried "No! Please! He's so young and must grow big and strong!"

The fawn said, "But I've just left my mother to build a home of my own, and I need something to eat."

"I'll lower my branch so you can eat at my house," said Mrs. Walnut.

And so she did!

One day Oscar heard a strange noise ripple through the meadow: it was laughter. A little boy and girl were happily running and and playing among the flowers and grass.

The little boy yelled, "Come on, Stephanie, let's climb this tree!" Oscar lowered his branch so they could climb up. "Oh, Wesley, what fun!", said Stephanie.

"What fun!" thought Oscar: he liked these two new creatures.

Suddenly, a mans' voice called to the children that it was time to go.

They ran off, promising Oscar that they'd return.

The next time Oscar saw his two little friends, they were with a woman and two men.

Wesley and Stephanie ran to play in Oscars' branches while the adults walked through the meadow and talked.

The man with the beard said they'd have to cut down "that tree".

"No!" cried the children. "We love this tree!" "I want a swing", said Stephanie. "And I want a tree house", said Wesley. "PLEASE!"

"PLEASE!" prayed Oscar.

"Well, it seems we'll have to find another place to build the house", said the father.

And so they did!

Oscar did indeed become the grandest walnut
tree in all the countryside!

G K Jones is an architect, builder, furniture maker, sculptor, and artist who studied at Long Beach State and UCLA. She did paintings for television shows and has many works in private collections. She has two children and three grandchildren, and currently lives with her three dogs in Arroyo Grande, California.

CPSIA information can be obtained
at www.ICGtesting.com
Printed in the USA
BVOW10*1928240316

441660BV00004B/4/P